HALLWAY CONFESSIONS

Also from Felicia C. Cade

Collected Pieces and Shed Skin

HALLWAY CONFESSIONS

Felicia C. Cade

Copyright © 2020 Felicia Cade

All rights reserved. No part of this book may be reproduced
or used in any manner without the prior written permission
of the copyright owner, except for the use of
brief quotations in a book review.

To request permissions, contact the publisher at f19cheri@gmail.com

Printed by Kindle Direct Publishing in the USA.

ISBN: 9798689236407

For Love
and all the wars we fight in between

For Her
the muse behind the mirror

For You
and all the depth of love you deserve

For Me
and all the courage it took to jump,
to stand, to stay, and sometimes, to leave

Find what has not been found

HALLWAY CONFESSIONS

Inhale   2
Break the Levee   3
So What   4
Inside View   5
War of Resistance   6
Mona Lisa   7
Who Hurt You?   8
Out of Breath   9
It Shows   10
Hallway Confessions   11
I Know   12
Open   13
Nothing Seems to Work   14
Triggered   15
It's A Lie   16
I Do   18

I'll Find You   19
Fall   20
You Deserve   21
Jenny   22
But If You Do...   23
Confrontation   24
Dear Love,   25
Stand Down   26
Give In   27
Confronting Constellations   28
Eye of The Storm   29
Something   30
She   31
Anyway   32
Maybe   33
Well   34
Her   35
Unfamiliar   36
Whole   37

DEEPER

Inside the Shell   43
They Will Say Things   44
This Deep   45
Searching   47
Guilty   48
Ghetto Might Save You   49
Strange Land   50
It's Changing You   51
Right There   52
Time Travel   53
Peter Pan   54
Poet   56
Good Women   57
Assume the Position   60
Close   61
This Ain't Checkers   62

You Choose   63
Black Cocaine   64
It's Changing You Pt. 2   65
Beyond the Casket   66
Duality   67
A Lie I Tell You   68
Lingua Franca   69
My Tongue Is...   70
Pride   71
Today   72
Internal Compass   73
Know God   74
Everything I Got   75
How   76
It Will Cost You   77
Optimized Illusions   78
Back to Adam   79
Watch Me   82
If You Let It   83

YOU NOT GON' KILL MY SON 84
Pray for The Pastor 85
When I See It 86
I Do 87
Forbidden Fruit 88
All 89
London 90
Ficus Pumila 91
Teeter Totter 92
Found 93
There Is an Eiffel Tower In You 94
Go 95
Casting Call 96
Audience of None 97
There Are Women Who Know 98
Touch the Past 99

Courage 100
Mirror, Mirror 101
Observe 103
Entanglement 104
Four You 105
Bore Not 106
Sensory Deprivation 107
Leave Him Be 108
Detached 109
The Last Message 110
Pandemic 111

Acknowledgments

Sometimes love leaves you in a hallway,
won't let you leave
and won't let you stay.

HALLWAY CONFESSIONS

Inhale

These walls are thin
And my thoughts are loud
Wrestling with things I'm too afraid
To speak
So I daydream
Go to a realm where freedom
Exists without consequence
And we fall at the same time
Catching each other's drifts
An entanglement of orbits
Nucleus and neutrons
Points penetrated and released
We breathe in unison
Inhale...

Hold...

Release...

Break the Levee

There is a levee between us
A thin wall holding back an ocean of secrets
And I'm not sure which is more dangerous
The breaking or the holding
The bursting forth or containing
I ask myself
Where is the freedom in this?
And if freedom was letting you go
Would I give?
Probably not
I want you to myself
And I don't want to share
I want your time, your energy
Your thoughts and your prayers

So What

And if I've made this whole thing
Up in my head, then I'm still
Blessed by just the thought of you

And what a thought you are
What an idea God had in mind
When He etched you into time

You are timeless
Beauty, wrapped in silence

Inside View

I crawled inside of you
Held for a moment what you've carried for a lifetime
And I wondered
How you managed
How you survived so long with so little
How you've kept a small patch
Of love and wonder
Hidden from a cruel world
That has never been kind to you
I collect the things that make you smile
For days when the hurt resurfaces
And you find it hard to not cry
I count your laughs
Place them in a jar
Use them to ease the anger
When you're triggered
Write you poems
For moments you're out of reach but not out of mind
And you are rarely out of mine
Rarely a thought I can escape
More like a path that flows in reverse
Rain that runs toward the clouds
Just to sit below the sun
You are God's favorite color
Even on days your paint bleeds off the page
And life exchanges your hard work for low wages
I just wish you could see you the way I do
But until you do
My eyes will always reflect your highest truth

War of Resistance

We exist somewhere
At some time
In some place
In some kind of reality
That does but doesn't exist
And I can't seem to unsee you
Unfeel you
Can't seem to tuck you away
Long enough to forget you
And I've tried
Flung myself into this war of resistance
And some days, I win
Other days, I'm drawn into your current
And I become defenseless
You are a mystery
A cave of dark secrets
Crying low enough to not be heard
But I hear you
Sit comfortably at the edge of your boundaries
And I don't even know how I got here
What led me to you
Why I keep stumbling at your door
In a slumber of emotions
Not sure what you have that I need
What you reflect
What truth is hidden under your wings
But I know it is strong enough to start a war

Mona Lisa

If beauty is in the eye of the beholder
Then I behold her
A perfect portrait painted to perfection
Drenched in divine dimensions
A cave of wonders
Get lost in her depths
Marvel at her diamonds
Trace her measurements
Find her secrets
Pour into her well
Watch light burst from her creases
Unframed
Untainted by past intruders
She is free
A collision of color leaks from her wings
Hypnotized by her song
Trapped in her maze
Pinned between her walls
I'm lost and not looking to be found

Who Hurt You?

I don't know who hurt you
Who swallowed you whole
And caged you in a maybe
Or tomorrow
You deserve to be a *right now*
A today
An impulse too strong to resist
I know you're worth the headache you give
That your lows are just as much a gift as your highs
You are a high
A trip in the mind
You take trips around my mind
Visit uninhibited areas and find me where
I have not been found
And I barely know your name
Or how you like your tea in the morning
If you even like tea in the morning at all
I just want to sit close enough for our knees to touch
Run my fingers through your thoughts
Give you rest
The kind that our souls search for
In unfit bodies that never seem to fit

Out of Breath

You, my dear

Are out of breath

And afraid to breathe...

It Shows

You have never been loved before and it shows
The way you search for a place
To store compliments
Hide from the world on days
When the sun is out

You have never been loved before and it shows
Never been touched with honest hands
Never been unraveled
Held beneath the bandages
Never had a safe place to lay your secrets
Allow your tears to Run.
Release.
Run.

You have never been loved before and it shows

Hallway Confessions

I'm only here because you called for me
Summoned me out of my slumber
Yet you treat me like a stranger
Like a guest you didn't expect
Closed the door in my face
Turned the lights out
In hopes that I would disappear
But do you really want me to disappear?
Do you really want me to crawl
Back into your subconscious
And fade back into a whisper?

Because I won't
I will sit in this hallway
Till you tell me to leave
Till those words crawl from your lips
And you look me in the eyes
Tell me you don't see me too
That you don't want this truth
At least for a little bit
That you ain't the least bit curious

I Know

See, I know something about you
That, despite the fear and hesitation
You love me too
Need me too
Just scared of all the noise
That may follow
Of what they will say
Of all the normal that I threaten
But normal is an illusion
A lie we paint for others' comfort
At the expense of our freedom to exist
So, we hold secrets for the sake of avoiding turbulence
Choke on predictable outcomes left in the hands
Of negative revisions that exist only in our Fears
When we could be free

Why don't we just be free?

Open

I hope you open yourself up
Wide enough and deep enough
To let your soul be penetrated
Let love enter your system
Fill all the cracks
Clear all the what-ifs
Leave you in a pool of bliss
Find solitude in watching you rest
On a bed of thoughts
That reflect how worthy
You have always been
I hope you don't miss your moment
That you break free from all that burdens you
That you open the curtains and let light touch your corners

Nothing Seems to Work

I've tried to erase you
Like legitimately forget you
Allow you to fade into my memory as
An infatuation birthed out of lonely
A thought I got carried away with
Gave myself that conversation you give yourself
When you feel like you're doing too much
I've tried to rationalize you out
Analyze how you got this close
And took up so much space in my mind
In such short a time
I tried to pray you away too
Link you to past trauma
A lesson and reflection
Sent for a reason and a season
But I can't seem to get you out
Claim my space and my thoughts back
Nothing seems to work
I'm back at this drawing board
Framing another escape
Haunted by your warmth
That still wraps around me in random moments
And I wasn't even looking for you
Walking my path
Minding my business
Fell into your cave of wonders
Fell victim to your spell and your scent
And I'm tired
So, I just let you sit on my conscience
Told myself that in time the thought of you
Would fade into the background
And life would resume as usual
But what is usual?

Triggered

It's the love that shows up
Unannounced that scares me
The one you never invited
Barges into your quiet dinner party
In full costume
Interrupts your entire routine
Triggers you like recycled trauma
Challenges all your boundaries
Twists the knobs on your secret compartments
And you hate it at first
Try and fight it
Silence it
But deep down something starts to happen
You start breathing
Realize that you were suffocating
In a reality that didn't fit
Question the need to protect perfect
The need to keep perfectly good china
Locked in a cabinet on display
Start to see with different eyes
Feel alive
Notice the clouds for the first time
And how your smile stretches a little wider than you thought
When real love hits you, it throws you completely off

It's A Lie

They say that love fades after a while
But it's a lie
You still look like the first day
And feel like the first time
You are a planet crowded by stars
A kiss too pure for lips
A campfire on a damp night
And your eyes tell stories
That make it hard to blink
You're a dream I can touch
A tangible love
In an artificial world

You are the longest poem
I have ever written a run-on
sentence chasing a period

I Do

I hate you
For the same reason that I love you
I guess I hate to love you
And love that I hate you

I'll Find You

You ain't gotta send me your location
Nor give me directions
I'll find you
In a million different galaxies
In a million different ways
Love you on every channel
Remove the clouds
On days when you want to see the sun
Plant seeds in your garden
For you to reap the harvest
Fight for your freedom
Carry your burdens
Find answers for your questions
And untangle your confusion

Fall

Fall into me
As I wrap myself in you
And let's stay there
Until we find home
Find peace
Find love jones on abandoned train tracks
Find rest
Explore each other's depths
See how deep trust can take us
How long we can stay naked
Before we search for covers

You Deserve

To be Seen
Found
Heard
Experienced
Explored
Loved

Until you burst into a thousand petals...
I hope you never settle

Jenny

She had a taste for disfunction
So, every now and then, she would leave to please it
Come back broken and low in spirit
And those days were the hardest
We just stayed silent
I removed the bandages
Cleaned the wounds she couldn't reach

I'm sure she wondered why I left the door open
Sometimes I did too
I suppose I understood her
Wanted her to know what home felt like in a human
How its arms are always open and without judgement
What love looks like on the other side of abandonment

But If You Do...

I know attachments
How they leach on
And take for selfish needs
Leave you empty
And drained
I know feelings
Short bursts of emotions
That fall into short flings
Just there for a good time
I know illusions
Imaginary images birthed out of lonely
And I am neither of the three
I am not lonely nor in need
Never had taste for short flings
Nor fantasy
But check for yourself
Feel my pulse
Search my eyes for intention
And if you do not find love, then leave
But if you do
Stay

Confrontation

You have something that I need
A truth deep enough to save me
But I'm afraid that I might drown
Before I reach your bottom
That I might get stuck between chapters
Or fall in love with running away with you
And the adventure of never having a destination
You make lost so appealing
Make pain appear less burdensome
Proof that company makes the dark less scary
But after a while our eyes adjust
Darkness doesn't seem so dark and the ticking
of the clock becomes faint
And we find ourselves in quicksand
Neither with enough strength to save the other
So we drown
Overdose on painkillers
We become the pain that killed us

Dear Love,

I'm scared too
Unprepared
Fragile and wounded
Confused
But you're worth it
Worth the fear I've had to face to find you
The lies that kept you out
The truth that binds us

Stand Down

Even if I never get to fully have you
I can say that I saw love once
Walked in its waters
Traced its palms
Listened to its stories
Sat inside its walls
Looked it in the eyes
And stood my ground
Remained resilient and unmoved

I fought for something
Gathered my gentle bones into one body
Forfeited all control

Give In

We know what we want
We always do
Truth ain't never hard to find
Just hard to digest
Hard to accept
That the plan won't always go as planned
No matter how hard we planned it
And love, be it a guest or a resident
Will always show up when you need it
And least expect it
It knows us
In ways we need to be known
And I don't know you
But I know you
Don't know what tomorrow holds
But today is hard to resist
I know I'm tired of fighting
And wearing clothes that don't fit
I know I'm too big for labels
I know that I love you
And all the chemicals that release in my head
When you come to mind
I know that love is hard to come by
I know that the hardest part of jumping is calculating the risk
And going within
I know that not jumping is a life half-lived
I know that happy is expensive
A high-class nigga with no regrets
I know that control is an illusion
And freedom, a choice

Confronting Constellations

She runs every time love comes close
Don't wanna be found
But hiding is getting heavy

She's afraid so she leaves herself behind
And gives into personified versions of herself
That she's created in other lovers
Costumes that are loose enough to fit into
But they get heavy too
Now she's pinned in a corner
A forced confrontation
As love sits pressed upon her chest
What will she choose?

Eye of The Storm

I am not afraid of tornados
I'll stand firm in the middle of your winds
And ride your waves
Till I find you again

I'm not afraid of your shadows
Nor your representative
Though his arrows are sharp
I know the truth that fuels him
And what's beneath

I know you want freedom just as badly as I do
But captivity is more appealing
A short ride that leaves a long high
But not all highs are the same
Most will leave just as fast as they came

Leave you heavy and uncovered
But I got you covered
Though you slay me with heavy stones
I hold my ground
Because love is a war that must be One

Something

Sometimes we cross paths with
Familiar strangers we've met before
Find question marks that lead to answers
for reasons that won't reveal themselves
Lest we surrender our comfort
Expose our dead leaves and sit
quietly on the edge until
Our terror runs cold and boldness turns
A whisper into a song not easily ignored
Find something we've looked for in others
But has always been at home
Something hard to define and difficult to deny
Too sacred to touch so we leave it
Admire its beauty without our fingerprints
Sit under monuments and above
Buried treasures that cause
A rumbling underground that few can hear
Lay our palms on the ground
Pressed against new grass
Calming Mother Earth
And centering ourselves
Finding rest in a hidden garden
Untouched by war
Letting tomorrow take care of itself
And freeing yesterday of its regrets

She

She is Everything
All that I am
And am not
A reflection of everything I've run from
And all that I am running to
We make sense
Together and apart
Make for a good conversation
And damn good art
Make for a reason to come out of hiding
To abandon it all

Anyway

I was stuck in grayscale
A stale cycle of repetition
But you came in color
A mystery of past pain and elusive beauty
I wanted to kiss you
Taste freedom on the tip of your tongue
Breath in your pain, exhale love in exchange
Help you find the pieces that you lost along the way
But life is a tricky game of reflections
The closer the image, the harder to see
So, we chase feelings
Grow dependent on heavy attachments
Just to find truths we already have
But can I touch you, anyway?
Sit in on a sober Saturday?
Ask questions that lead us deeper into this pool?

Maybe

Maybe you are an illusion
A romanticized idea
An exaggerated truth
An altered reality where
Everything is bliss and all
Things work in perfect harmony
A desire birthed in dry land

Or maybe you are real
Maybe I'm right about everything I feel
Maybe the heart is deceitfully wicked
And I've been blinded by shadows buried deep in my mind
Maybe you are a reflection of whispers I've been
too afraid to speak out loud

I don't know, but I need to know
Can't spend any more time
Twirling my thumbs
Or holding my breath
Tryna figure this out

Tell me who you are?

Well

Love abandoned me
Lured me to the river and left me thirsty
Stripped me naked and left me exposed
Wide open with no covering for my internal organs
In an audience of our choosing
Then faded behind the scenes
But I bore the shame
Absorbed the pain
Covered myself in leaves
Sat in the groove of an old oak tree
And wept till I was free
Stitched the wounds that were still open
Crafted armor strong enough to protect me
Yet gentle enough to breathe
And held no anger in my heart
Though her rage would be justified
Decided that I would not let pain
Make a slave of me so I forgave
Without an apology or explanation
Found a new path with more sunshine
And continued on my journey

Her

Men have always disappointed me
Always sought to seek themselves first
Have always been destructive and careless
Always seen me flesh-first
And Women have always picked up where they left
Always cleaned up their mess
Always considered the well-being of his guest

So, when I see love, I see it in them
In the gentleness and honesty of their eyes
In the service of their hands
In the warmth of their voice that comes in
Clear on days that the earth is shaking

In the kitchen, cooking meals that
Ease hunger and heartbreak
In her feet, and all the miles it takes
To walk on fire without burning
The tips of her dress

When I see love, I see it in her

Unfamiliar

Two sides of the same mirror
Fighting for a clearer picture
Running through a forest of
Translucent shadows
Looking for something stable
Somewhere to hide
From all the unfamiliar

Whole

If I could describe this love
I wouldn't
For it speaks a language
That doesn't speak at all
It just knows
And you just know
That nothing has ever felt so...

Ever had the power to slow
The world down inside your mind?
You wake up crying, trying to figure
How you got so lucky...wonder
How you went so long without it
Fear the day that you will have to live without it
And it takes time to adjust to its power
Gather all that it has exposed
Give it permission to overtake you
Without fear of drowning

Then you rest in its arms and realize
What safe really is—how whole
Home should have always been

Find what has not been found...

DEEPER

Felicia C. Cade

Inside the Shell

There is a you
That exists inside of you
Right underneath the you
You present to the world
But you hide it
For it is fragile and unbalanced
Impulsive and reckless
It loves hard, heavy
Is vulnerable, easily broken
If mishandled
Still learning its power
It's afraid of falling and not
Having the strength to get back up
But you always get back up, don't you?

They Will Say Things

They will say things
Nothing to do with you
More to do with who they are
What you make them see
In themselves
They will say things

Empty sentences full of words they have not weighed
Have not seasoned with love and understanding
Understanding don't say too much
Doesn't have to speak what is already known
For love is a sweet talker that knows your spot
And when God speaks, it lifts a burden, settles the turmoil

Pay them no mind, Child
Keep dancing to your rhythm
Boldly sway those hips
Like you've got lessons hidden in 'em
Smile
You've got every reason to

Let insults fall like dead leaves
Pave your path to you
To heights their voice can't reach
Oh My Child, they will say things
But your blessings will be too loud
Not to notice

This Deep

Love this deep will drown you
In everything you think you are not
If you are not ready
So I get why they run from me
Why they hide from Love
Why they settle for surface touch
While their soul is naked
Midwinter cold
In need of warmth

But I cannot get why
I leave summer to freeze in your cabin
Why I feel you like I feel me
Why I risk my own safety to reach into your fire
To save you

I don't know
Maybe I secretly want to be saved too
Brought out of the dark of isolation
And pushed into a sea of possibilities
Maybe I give what I don't have

Hope as if, one day, it will show up for me
Love as if, one day, it will show up for me

I pour into bottomless wells
And cry when there is no return
This must be some kind of insanity
Some kind of sick game
I play on myself
Must be some kind of hell my
Grandmother bought and forgot to pay

And I just don't know how much more my heart can take
If I can bear the weight of any more broken men
At the expense of my peace of mind
And I wonder if daddy knew his absence
Would create a generation of broken
Children breaking each other
Trying to find him
Sometimes, I wonder if daddy knew
How important he was and still is

Searching

I suppose I'm searching
for what I have always been searching for
I want Truth
No matter which parts of myself
I must burn

Guilty

These tears are for those I have crushed
In the instability of my adolescence
Whipped with my judgement
Swallowed in the heat of my anger
These tears are my own
Made of mistakes I can never take back
And words I can never un-say
For the revenge I still want
And the unforgiveness
That has made me bitter
These tears are the heaviest that
My eyelids have ever bled
But they are necessary
For, how can I accuse
My oppressor of his sins while
There's still blood on my hands?

Let me be for awhile
Let me mourn in peace
Let me carry this guilt
Till I've studied its weight
Gathered its lessons and found
The root of its pain

Ghetto Might Save You

I've been quiet when I wanted to scream
Allowed my boundaries to be fucked with
And energy to be drained
All in the name of love
A love that I have never given myself
And I regret it
Wish I would've allowed my anger to have its way
Flipped the table on injustice
Left him naked in a bed suffocating on his own lies
Pulled a Bernadine
Threw all his shit in a Volvo and lit it on fire
But I done trained myself to be civilized
Convinced myself I'm not ghetto like Titi and them
When ghetto done saved more women than it has harmed
I know that black women love differently
We spin yarn into gold
Use every part of our emptiness to give what we never got
Invest time, money, and energy
Carrying his baggage and dirty secrets
All while they spit in our faces
Use us for their needs
Run our bodies dry
And then leave

Strange Land

At my center
I am fragile
Quiet and humble
I spend most of my time in thought
Pondering the human experience
As if I am something different
A visitor in a strange land
Passing time
Dusting off the beauty
That man has trampled on and forgotten
I am fascinated with trees
I can stare at them for hours
Something about the strength in their roots
And the gentleness of their leaves
Brings me peace and leaves me in wonder
But it's not long before
My primal needs call me out of center
And back to the village
Where I must hunt for food
And congregate with others
I dread it
There are no trees there
The lights are bright
It is loud
The ground is covered in dark rock
And the villagers have become aggressive
Predators with no regard for each other
They are prisoners of habit
And have blocked out moon
To make their own light
But one day soon, center will be my home
And I will be back among the trees where I belong

It's Changing You

She hurt you
And you're still standing in that same spot
Questioning yourself
Holding back an ocean of tears
Trying to sex your way out of not feeling like enough
Making your bed a crime scene
Of innocent bystanders
Because you gave her all you had
But it still wasn't enough
And that hurt has changed you
Given way to a graveyard of innocent women
And it's all catching up to you
Turning your reflection into an image
That is beginning to look less and less like you

Oh Brother, I beg of you
To free the women in bondage to you
To close your bedroom
Until you weep,
Until you release
And I promise you
Love will come again
Just as deep and just as loud
Only this time, it will stay

Right There

I wanna get under your skin
Behind the thoughts that keep you up at night
I wanna know the blankets of trauma that replay
In your subconscious
I wanna speak to the thing that hurts the most
Rub my fingers through your insecurities
And love you like you have never been loved before
Love you for all the days sorrow has stolen
Love you so good and so deep
That you feel unworthy and undeserving
You cry for no reason
But you take it in
Hold me in your lungs
Till they burst open
And you become a new creature
Not bound by breath
And life begins to look different

Time Travel

I am time
And I don't have minutes to waste
I have my own pace
Run too fast, you will lose me
Run too slow, I will pass you by
But if you get in rhythm with me
We can dance in a realm
Where minutes and seconds
Stop just to marvel at us

Peter Pan

I'm everything you asked for but didn't expect
Now you a shaky shooter with a bounced check
Guess your eyes were bigger than your stomach
Game got too heavy you called a forfeit
Fumbled before the touchdown
But I'm used to it
And this will be the last time
I pull out the good China for a cheap guest
Cause every time you invest in potential
You enter into never neverland
And Peter Pan might not ever wanna
Leave never neverland
So sis you gotta level up
Pick your chin up
Find the highest you
Wear her over the make-up
And suddenly the sea gets a little clearer
Fish a little bigger
Bon appétit
Kings recognize Queens
And act accordingly
Never inconsistent or with the foolery
You become a major priority
Imagine that
He never breaks a promise or forgets to text you back
You cooking him dinner and rubbing his back
Real recognize real and that a fact
We done loved too hard
To not get it back
Wasted too many glasses of good wine
On untangling lies, spending time that we can't get back
Sista, if you hearing this
Know that he will never change unless

He encounters God or tragedy hits
But he got 15 different God's that all look like him
And tragedy is a gamble that might never hit
So, let this be the last time that
You're reminded
You deserve more than this
Take this confirmation and run with it
Until the man across your dinner table
Is a reflection of what Love had in mind
When it created you

POET

We are not an underground art
A Hobby or pastime
A space filler for musical acts
A shhhh and "Don't say that"
We are not rappers
Playing word games for your entertainment
We ain't no nick nack patty wack give a few Bars and raps for a few claps
We are not for free, nor are the words we enslaved in the trenches of life
We are the MOUTH of GOD,
Prophets and Scribe holders,
Truth tellers,
And soul healers, miracle workers
And peacemakers

Good Women

When men get their heart broken
They use good women to mend it
Dump all of they junk into her spirit
Then uses her body to get high with
You know until he's had his fix
Then he Tosses her aside
Once the guilt sets in

Now she's left broken
Emotionally broke and open
Vulnerable for attack
Vultures hunting for wounded women
And she gets swept up before
She even had time to breathe in

Now she gets high to numb the feeling
Womb full of mixed semen
Seeds of demons
Grow into mental cages
Now they calling her crazy
Drowning and in need of saving

She went to church that evening
But it was after hours
Tried to call the office but no answer
didn't have the words to leave a message
So she took one last hit
And fell asleep on the steps

But little did she know
She wouldn't see morning
She overdosed
Now her mother is mourning

But he didn't mean to
Didn't expect his actions to have reactions
Now he's overreacting
Trying to find a place to tuck the guilt in
But he's outta options

Stuck with the same heart that started it
And I'm not sure where this cycle ends
Or who's to blame

But I know that fathers are supposed to
Set standards and protect they daughters
And fathers are supposed to mold boys into men

So I suppose neither of them really had a chance
What a tragic end...

A lesson to men
Sex won't heal your heart
And every woman after her
Shouldn't have to suffer for the shit you won't sit in silence for
You better find a way to cry boy
Let that well run dry boy
Till you can see with clear eyes boy

A message to women
Careful who you open your temple to
Lest you inherit more demons
Than you're accustomed to
Daddy won't protect you
So you better
Spirituality and mentally
Tune in
Use your intuition and discernment
Lest you end up somebody wasteland and servant

Now back to your regular scheduled programming

Assume the Position

You see yourself in everything
Which is why you never see anything
Explains why you lack perspective
Avoid mirrors of introspection
Can't recognize your voice
From strangers'
You get lost in opinion
Lack the ability to allow thought to exceed emotion
So you assume conclusions
Leaving you ass-deep on the wrong end

Close

I wanna be written into his morning routine
Carved into his bed like good linen
Pressed into his couch
Palms permanently stained on his countertops
I want him under covers and above
Want his thoughts tethered into mine
Wanna be glued to his side

This Ain't Checkers

I don't respond to what doesn't apply to me
I control my energy
And keep a force field around my synergy
Double stomp on these haters like Quan Chi
Dismiss foolery like a disease
Drama free 7 days a week
Grounded like an old willow tree
A truth teller I be
Lover of all things pure
Tuned in to everything black and relevant
Sensitive but sensible
Gentle but not gullible
A chess player, nigga
Know ya role

You Choose

Victim of circumstance
Or Villain dodging consequence
You choose
Cause every villain had a childhood
And every victim has a choice
And reality is a short nigga with no filter
You choose
Tell me what sin defiles a man more
Than the lies he tells himself
And who's protecting the children
Recording the secrets of our elders
Tell me why we are still in character
Long after the play has ended
Why we still whisper the shit
Our heart is screaming
Locking ourselves in cubicles
Chained to false perceptions of adulthood
Selling our time for paychecks
Chasing deadlines and distractions
Giving purpose to the loose nipple that barely got milk

Black Cocaine

Cocaine was our first pandemic
A hard rock and a cold killer
Ran through black bodies like cancer
Swallowed up childhoods like
Unforgiving black holes
Packed and sold
Planted in the hood
Baited and hooked
A decent price for a short high
Panic attacks and paranoia
Drug dealers stealing hope from they own
To make a quick buck
Dead bodies hung over kitchen tables
Babies born as fiends barely breathing
They deemed it a
WAR ON DRUGS
It was really a
WAR ON US
A reason to kill and bag us up
Break our homes
Kill our hope
Paint us publicly uncivil
To justify their evil
Lock us in cages
Create a new plantation
With low wages
Then burn the evidence
Call it a conspiracy theory
Claim innocent until proven guilty
Deem us crazy
Turn truth into an exaggeration

Its Changing You Pt.2

He hurt you
And you want revenge
Want him to pay for everything he did
And you've been holding that gun
In your hand for years
Fighting the tears
Cause he ain't worthy of 'em

But that pain is changing you
That flame you holding is beginning to burn through your skin
Sister, I beg of you
Put the anger down and allow your tears to cleanse you
And I promise you that the woman behind this wall will find herself new
Will prove that ashes are the birthing ground for warrior
Women who have Survived attacks powerful enough
To level an army of men
Oh Sister, I beg of you
Don't let this heavy cloud stop
Your sunshine from breaking through

Beyond the Casket

There will be no secrets to tell at my funeral
No words I did not say
No ex-lovers who will speak ill of my name
No work I left undone
Just a story
Of how a weird little black girl
Found her power
And used it for good
Of how God uses ordinary people
For extraordinary things

When my casket closes
It will echo across the world
The sun will weep
The ground will receive me with joy

And my spirit will finally stretch out in all its fullness

Duality

I Love the simplicity of men
And the complexity of women
His strength and power
Her vulnerability and sensuality
Both beautiful in their own light
Both a reflection of the duality of my own essence
And God's nature
And I don't know where love will take me
But I know that truth has always fought to find me
I know that I don't have to know today
I know that God is enamored
By my boldness to silence expectations
And ask hard questions
I know I'm not afraid of the dark
Nor intimidated by the light
Which makes me a force to be reckoned with

A Lie I Tell You

Traveled across the water
To find what was NOT here all along
It's a lie I tell you
Sometimes home is too small to hold you
Too familiar to appreciate your value
Too slow to catch the drift
A half-step back
And hard relapse
Sometimes, home is quicksand
A land of sunken ships and lost dreams
A matrix of mind games and trickery
A prison of broken adults
And screaming children fighting for attention

Lingua Franca

I speak different languages
Reach past the ear
And under the conscience
Dabble in the fragile space
That humans hide
And although I am sometimes ignored
I am always understood
Always a well of wealth
To those who choose
To be still enough for an exchange

My Tongue Is...

A problem solver and a shit starter
A revolving channel of divine knowledge
A hot topic
A fully loaded automatic
A barrier-breaking
Burst from the womb and be free conversation
A smooth criminal with good intentions
A sweet kiss and nibble on the bottom lip
A whisper and announcement
A word of wisdom to the wise
A puzzle to un-illuminated minds
A too late and an on-time
A tongue twister
Go getter
Double clutch
Heavy hitter
Young spitter
Slanging scripture to these Hitlers

Pride

And what have you come to prove?
What fragile have you come to cover?
What words have you come to steal?
What tears do you refuse to release?
Who told you that strength isn't having
The courage to feel it all?
To be brave enough?
To love at the bottom of a fall?
To say your truth and keep your power?
Who said that pride wasn't the weak one?

Today

Yesterday is gone
And tomorrow will not come
Until you conquer today
And today will repeat herself
Till she is heard
And is not the future
A reward for all the todays
You had the courage to conquer?

Internal Compass

I am a wanderer
But I am never lost
Though my path may not be straight nor planned
There is a map
A compass that is never out of tune
I do not pack before I journey
But I am never without
Food or shelter
I do not anticipate war
But I have never lost a battle

Know God

I Know God
He knows me
And it's this knowing that keeps us knitted
We have no secrets
No topics off limits
Not confined by religious barriers
That once made us strangers
We just exist
In each other
And even when I'm stubborn
And carve my own images
Out of past traumas
He calls my bluff
Shows up at my dinner party
And just stares at me
Until my eyes swell up
And truth falls from my lips
Heart lay bare
Exposed like dry bones
And for a moment
I escape this body and all its weight
Become, once more, atom and light
Taste Eden before disruption
Roam naked in a garden
That bears fruit in all seasons
Sing a melody that has no ending

Everything I Got

I want Your spirit to break out in me
Pull these weeds up from the root
I'm tired of weekend visits
I want You to move in
Set up permanent residence at the seat of my heart
I want You to eliminate my subconscious
Till every wicked thought is exposed
I want to be one with You
Conjoined
Tangled up
Shackled at the ankles
Till my bones fade back to dust
And I meet You in the clouds
Press my thumbs in the wounds of Your wrist
Kiss Your feet
Feel your glory pass by me
Expand my human capacity
So that I can have more of You
I want to see what this world has never seen
Want to be cleaned out enough
To be a Transair of miracles
Want to be drunk off Your spirit
High off the sound of Your voice
Addicted to Your presence
Break every curse plaguing my generation
Want to be a direct reflection of my abba
And I'll pay whatever it cost
Give up everything that I got

How

I'm tired of marching
Tired of black mothers screaming
Maybe we should hang you
Hunt you for sport
Leave your boys in pools of blood
Blame it on a hoodie and pack of skittles
Put a gun to your head
Long enough for you to consider death
Pollute your water
Lock up your fathers
Maybe we should burn down your neighborhoods
While dressed in black sheets
See if you're really human
If you've got a pulse and a soul
See if you bleed as we do
Feel pain and remorse like we do
Because sometimes I wonder
How so much evil could exist inside of a body so deeply
That it leaks through generations...
If you know who you are without all that hate...

It Will Cost You

When you move lies in, they become truth
And it's not long before
You're stuck in a version of yourself
That ain't you
Band-aids are only good for temporary use
To protect new wounds
Use them as long-term solutions and they cause infection
Follow directions
Don't get tangled up in your own clouded perception
Don't use confusion as a way to protect your addictions
Face your demons
Be careful where you place your semen
Be watchful of the company you keep
It takes the same energy to run in a circle
As it does a straight line
It would be wise
To not waste time

Optimized Illusions

I was scared
But couldn't give my fears a voice
So, I found myself swinging in the dark
Missing targets
Losing energy
Until the light came on
And I realized
The room was empty
I had been fighting illusions
Blinding myself to hard truths
Cause I didn't want to give up my lies
They had grown on me
Wrapped themselves around my skin
Made me a runaway dreamer
With cold feet
My reflection was still blurry
Covered in debris of past storms
And hurt that my tears couldn't wash away
Dodging a future that was bigger than today
A forever that was so close
It seemed far away
Cause I didn't feel worthy enough to hold it
To lead and nurture this newborn truth
But still it grew strong enough to hold its own

Back to Adam

I could see it in her eyes
It was deeper than sex
She wanted me to be her God
To validate her beauty
And momentarily calm her insecurities
She wanted her depths explored
To be unraveled
To take her clothes off
And lay her fears down
She just wanted to be loved
And I did too
Adored
Kissed until the hurt faded away
She wanted to be free
But somewhere along the line
Freedom became a distant dream
Too many false prophets and crooked Kings
Making extravagant promises only to
Get in her palace and steal her jewels
And for a moment, I wanted to be that for her
For the me in her
To kiss her back to life
To untie her knots
Let her walls down so she could
Breathe for awhile
Because I know what suffocating feels like
What the weight of a man's lies and inconsistency can do to you
What being put on hold can do to your heart
And how it can exhaust your mind
It was more than an orgasm that we wanted
It was being loved so deep
That your body cries

It was being loved so deep that you surrender
Wave your white flag, let your gun down
And surrender...
But I remember
That thou shalt not lay with a woman
As she would a man
For a reason
I remember
That I cannot save her, just as much as I cannot save myself
And we cannot hide for long
In this forbidden garden before we start to bleed again
I remember that we are not doctors
Just patients trying to help each other
Bear the pain
Cover the wounds until God finds His way
Through our cluttered and crowded rooms
So instead of sex
We chose to just sit
To interlock hands and cry
Wipe each other's tears
And just breathe together
We realized
That breathing together
In the dark felt better than
Hiding from the light
We traded an orgasm for freedom that night
And I chose to return to my Adam

Because I love you
Despite what you have done Adam
I am still bone of your bone
And flesh of your flesh
But it seems you have forgotten that
And I cannot un-belong to you
Without making humanity suffer

We are waiting on you Adam
Where are you?
Can you hear your rib calling out to you?

Watch Me

Watch me run
Like the race is already mine
Watch me fly
Like the wind is following my lead
Watch me be black
Dark like the sun was made for me
Watch me dangle my feet in the promised land
And watch God do what He say
Watch Love crash into me like a wave
Watch me free my momma
And all her children who became slaves
Watch me smile
Like the edges of my mouth got something to tell my ears
Watch me cry like it's my strength
Watch me be
Like your opinion never mattered
Watch me dance
Like nobody's watching
Watch me
Cause I deserve to be watched
And watch me watch you
Like you matter
Like I see greatness leaking out your future
Like you got an army of angels behind you
Like you can't be covered
Ignored
Pushed aside
Like you too big of an idea to be quiet
You better say something
Say it loud too
Bet it echoed around mountains and into tombs
Bet your voice open doors than your hands can't

If You Let It

You deserve consistency
A love that rises with the sun
And falls in its proper order
I am a wildflower
A wind chaser lost in freedom
Skipping along an ever-winding road and our love is a mystery
A place where freedom and containment meet
And we wrestle
You fight to contain my winds
I fight to loosen your restraint
While truth sits in the middle
A vortex of divine intervention
A reflection of puzzle pieces
Trying to piece together a perfect picture

Love will change you if you let it
Why don't we let it?
Why do we run
From the ones we pray into existence?
Maybe we like the chase
The fun of the game
The seeking and the hiding

Promise you'll never stop seeking me
That, if this game ends
You will still set me free
Find me in new places
Promise you won't clip my wings
Or place boxes around my dreams
Promise me that love won't try and fix me
That it will accept as I am
When it is all said and done

YOU NOT GON' KILL MY SON

I hope you swallow every bullet
Lodged in the back of black boys
I hope the dead come find you in your sleep
And you wake up every morning to the sound of
Screaming mothers
I hope you suffer
I hope the bones in your knees dismantle
And you spend the rest of your days crawling
Like the snake you are
I hope justice lands you behind bars
For every playdate George will miss with his daughter

How dare you tell me how angry to be
Or how loud to scream
With gun to my head and knee in my throat

How dare you tell me to pray
Like God ain't weighed my tears and seen my pain
These poems is prayers
Is songs of distress in troubled times
Is century-old hymns
Is power
And faith in the face of Goliath
With the head of a lion
These poems is politically correct
Is a movement hovering over America
Like a hurricane of justice
Black gon' matter
Or she gon' swallow the earth whole with no remorse

Pray for the Pastor

The world wants blood
Wants you to pay for the sins of those who lied
In the name of Jesus
They want your head, Pastah
For all religious leaders who lead the flock into the land of
Greed and illusion
And church folk got you by the throat
Want you to be superhuman
Holy and pure
Perfect and motionless
They will praise you for works that are not of your doing
Hang on your every word
Grow deaf to the God you speak of
And when you fall
Both the world and the church will crucify you
But you will still pray for them
On death beds and, at 3am
Christen their babies
Find a sermon on days when you need one yourself
Find a way to be thoughtful and kind

You must really serve some kind of God
That must be real
Because no amount of money
Could convince a man
To spend his life serving between two worlds that
Have their swords drawn and their hands out

When I See It

Men have always disappointed me
Always sought to seek themselves first
Have always been destructive and careless
Always seen me flesh first
And Women have always picked up where they left off
Always cleaned up their mess
Always considered the well-being of his guest
So, when I see love
I see it in them
In the gentleness and honesty of their eyes
In the service of their hands
In the warmth of their voice that comes in clear
On days that the earth is shaking
In the kitchen
Cooking meals that ease hunger and heartbreaks
In her feet and all the miles they take her
To walk on fire without burning the tips of her dress
When I see love I see it in her

I Do

Body wanted it
Mind thought of too many
Unfavorable conclusions
Wondered if I could get the orgasm
Without getting my heart tangled
Surely God would understand
Sometimes a woman has needs that prayer can't fix
Because I been praying
And Craving skin like water
And he look like a good time
Like he knows all the right buttons
And hell, I just might

Forbidden Fruit

You love me
Your eyes tell on you
But I will keep your secret
Won't utter a word
If you don't want me to
Keep my eyes closed
So you don't have to face this truth
But how long do you think you can keep this up?

All

I might abandon it all
Just to touch you
Feel the depth in your cracks
And the warmth in your silence
Cause I ain't never seen such beauty up close
A galaxy of small combustions of light
You make temptation feel right
Got my moral compass
Fighting to find direction
I want you soul-deep

Want to peel away lies that cage your smile
   "Your Smile"
The way the edges of your mouth
Push joy out of your eyes
   "Your Eyes"
Cradle stories and buckle knees
You make sentences hard to form
Letters get confused
Words get tangled up

And I'm not strong enough to resist you
Not evil enough to dress you in my selfish needs
I just watch you

London

Something about the confidence in your voice
The way you carry rainy days like sunshine
The revelations that run through tube stations
And how you put milk in your tea

I think I'm in love...

How you don't speak much
But when you do
Intelligence puts this red dress on and tells
Stories in ways that keep me engaged
Something about your secrets
How you tuck them beneath your collar
Something about the way you protect old wisdom
And embrace new ideas
Something about Brixton
The way you breathe in seasons
And let your hair down on Saturday evenings
Something about your art and your accent that just feel right
Something about your culture
A melting pot of potent roots that blend just right
Something about your closeness and small rooms
Basements and rooftops
Pubs and graveyards
Something about you

Ficus Pumila

Suffocating in a garden of flowers
Swallowed by weeds that wrap around roots
Steal sunshine from the palm of her petals
Drain her of all the labor
She has gathered for her debut
Strip her stem of the song rushing up her throat
She is dying at the hands of those
She sacrificed her sunshine for

And she still won't cry
Won't surrender
Wont curse the weeds or winds
Though they slay her

For freedom she earned with honest prayers
They've got a taste for blood, I tell you
Gon' kill that girl in cold blood, I tell you
Watch her dreams dry up
Burn her remains
But they gon' regret it
Gon' realize: if the sun dies
It takes the moon with it

Teeter Totter

You push me out
I pull you in
Gravity anchors us
In truths we didn't expect
Spins us in circles
As we try to resist
And we both want out
So we run in opposite directions
But never win
End up exhausted and out of breath
Stretched out and mentally deaf
I suppose the lesson is this:
"You can run from love
But you can't run from yourself"

Found

I have found God
At the bottom of my sorrow
And the edge of my bitterness
Found Him deep
Pressed against church walls
Above polished ceilings
Found myself, too
And although I'm a little less clean than I thought
His love is still the same and His blood makes up
For everything I am not

I have found God
And not the one my grandmother hid in her closet
on days she decided to be evil
Found Him on street corners, hanging out
In the hearts of rebels
In elevated rooms, having enlightened conversations
Found Him in the comfort of a stranger
And the resilience of my mother
Found Him in places they said He was not
Guess the saying is true
What you see is dependent on what you're looking for

There Is an Eiffel Tower in You

There is an Eiffel Tower in you
And I hope you find it
Climb it
Touch its peak
Sit and soak
In a higher amplitude
Hope you don't get lost at the bottom
Where it's crowded
Full of onlookers with opinions
Blaming conditions
Hope you light up in your darkest hour
That the nights you survived become
A combustion of light that launches you into sight
I hope you find it
That you don't die average
Don't pass through this world
As another body
Packed with boundless potential
I hope time is merciful to you
That you find the courage
To plant yourself in proper soil
And that you chase the son (sun)
Bask in rays till you radiate
Till you vibrate so high
That the room shakes

Go

When you don't know which direction to go
Know this
The direction is always forward
Always away from pain
And bondage
Always towards love
Always towards God
Always the path with the most peace
Know that you can control the sails
But not the direction of the winds nor
The heights of the waves

Casting Call

Men have a picture
A role they want you to play
In their movie
And most women put on the costume
Leave themselves behind
And play the role
Till they can no longer
Distinguish between the character
And their reflection
And the movie always changes
Always has a weird plot twist
That leaves her in the deficit

Audience of None

If your confidence is built on applause
What happens when the clapping Stops?

There Are Women Who Know

There are women who know
Know things they shouldn't know
Know that knowing won't help
But you can't unknow what you know
You know
They just know
When and how
What and where
Know just how much seasoning is missing
Know how long to hug you
Know where it hurts
And no one knows how they know
But they know that too
There are women who know

Touch the Past

I've touched the past
Sat in the blood of my ancestors
Listened to their screams
From the bottom of a dungeon
Where they were packed, 300 wrapped
In blood, sweat and fear
I've rubbed my fingers across their scars
Sat in their darkness
Seen the reality of today
Long hours that pour into the night
A day's work for an hour's pay
That's barely enough to buy bread and water
So you choose between two needs
Pray for some kind of relief
And a word from God costs, too
Because pastor preaching, but he hungry too
Spirit willing, but his flesh is starving
And tomorrow ain't looking too promising
Politicians with no vision
And a government with no system
Little faith and a lot of religion
So, I ask myself: how far are we from freedom
If our mother is being strangled
And we are too busy buying sneakers?
How far are we from freedom
If we know not who we are?
How far are we from freedom now?
Tell me so I can relay the message to our children
That maybe we were too selfish to see
Too busy to fight
And too scared to die

Courage

And if we don't heal
We become the missing pieces
A collection of coping mechanisms
A playground of escapism
Spells of depression
Moral decay that filters through our system
Till we become bitter, broken, and bruised
Heavy and misused
Reality, an unwelcome guest
Warning us of how unforgiving time is
And our children become infected
With all the demons that snuck in
Through the cracks we left open
While running
From everything we had the courage to face
And I hope you face it
Close every wound your mother left
And door your father left open
Find the courage to fight generational wars
Before the pain begins to show up on your face
And guilt greets you at an old age
As we see blessings we missed along the way
And the destruction we left behind

Mirror, Mirror

I've been programmed on how to see my own reflection
Injected with images of who I am
Based on their perception
Social rejection
And we believed them
Watched them portray us
As criminals and loose cannons
Deem us untamed
To justify their enslavement
Starved and put in a cage with my brother
Till one of us got hungry enough to kill the other
We surviving out here
War vets with shell shock
Bullets and helicopters
Incarcerated behind steel doors
With no windows
Fighting for sanity
Tears of blood
Bleeding behind porcelain images
Because rent don't care about your feelings
Angry, with no room for expression
Because being Black in America is a terrorist threat
Traumatized by images of black boys rotting on concrete
At the hands of officers who just felt like proving something
Dropped in a foreign land to breastfeed the same children
Who would soon whip us until our bones separated from flesh
But their 400 years is up
What they thought they buried wasn't dead
Should have checked the pulse
For the last shall be first
And we shall arise new
Burst through heaven's gates with a song
Nappy hair and all:

Ain't You

Ain't You tired, Mas'a
Of all this death?
All these bodies in your closet and blood on your rug
Ain't you tired, Mas'a
Of all these devils running round yo head?
In yo fields and in your bed
Do you really need to own niggas that bad?

Ain't you tired of suffocating your conscience
Holding all that evil in your organs?

Observe

An outsider
Of a world that doesn't make sense
A circus of mutual entertainment
As the audience falls into the same scene
That the actors are enslaved to

Entanglement

We lie to ourselves
Paint a white fence around an idea of love
And box ourselves in
Play the part
Wear the dress
Wear the pants
Show up for the show
But eventually the audience disappears
The light zeroes in
And we find ourselves not in love
But "IN' an idea
And so far outside ourselves
We forget who we are
And what it feels like to feel
Then a feeling comes along
Wrapped in a reflection of familiar pain
And we get entangled
Try to save ourselves by saving someone else
Because we all want freedom
But freedom is a threat to a bird without wings

For You

I held you in my arms
Watched life leave your body
Grazed my hand over your eyes
And felt a cold whisper wash over you
Tears ran into screams
Enough anger to kill an army
Enough tears to flood a forest

A piece of me died with you
Went cold and dark
Found it difficult to talk to God without yelling
So I stopped talking

I couldn't protect you
Would have jumped in front of a bullet to see
Your dreams come true
It was too soon
Bitterness overtook me
And your tomorrows still haunt me

I need prayer
The kind that got pastor speaking in other languages
This pain ain't gon' leave me
Till justice is screamed from mountain tops

Bore Not

You held me underwater
Watched me gasp for air
Brought me to the surface
Just before my lungs caved in
You seemed to like to dangle me
Between life and death
Force fed me your sorrow
Because someone had to pay
Crucified for sins that I bore not
But it only made me stronger
My resurrection, a little sweeter
Bones a little more stable in structure
A little less afraid of the edge

Sensory Deprivation

Reality has always been a haze
A cloud of disproportionate complexities
Thick fog hovering over open lakes
Love being the only time that my senses return
The only thing strong enough to ground me
I rest there when I can
Taste what I have not seen
Touch what I have not heard
Take deep breaths
And long pauses
Allow my senses to grab
What they can of the moment
Before it passes

Leave Him Be

Rushing everywhere yet arriving
Nowhere at the same time
Blinded by his own reflection
He emits light
Only to cast shadows
He is a lie
A half-truth past noon
A passive transaction
And empty deposit
Leave him be
Let him rot in his own vomit
Till he can stomach himself
Be not a doormat of palate pleasers
Guilty of treason
Lest you end up a clown
In his circus of optical illusions
You are not a game
To be opened and played
For entertainment
Let him be I say
Before he steals time you ain't got to spare
And energy you ought not waste

Detached

Miss my days of detachment
When my heart was tucked in
And the world was a non-biased observation
Humans are always inconsistent and fallible
Needy and unreliable
Hardly stay still in love long enough to be touched
Wasted orgasms and empty hands hold
Each other's loss of hope in something deeper
Shame creeps in like a Pentecostal pastor
With no mercy for the sinner
Trying to gather the courage I've got left
To break past this levee
Ask God questions I don't want the answers to
Bitterness holds justice for withheld judgement on
Intruders plucking innocence before its time
Just need time to sort it out
Feel my feelings without logic making a mockery of me
I knew better. We always know better
But isolation be making compromising arrangements
And the heart chooses who it chooses
Without considering your considerations
Like a kid that speaks his mind at the wrong time
And you're stuck apologizing for honest comments
Wish we all could be more honest

The Last Message

You will search for me and come up empty
Settle for pieces of me scattered
Among random women
Pussy gon' get old to you at a young age
And you gon' want something deeper
But you won't find it
And all the women you used along the way
Will have found themselves out of your cage of validation
And you will end up alone
A different kind of alone, though
The empty kind that's too much to bear
But somehow you make it to the next day

Pandemic

They say it's a pandemic
But I say it's a global reset
A chance for all the little voices to be heard
Can you hear them?
Mother Earth breathing for the first time
Children playing catch on the front lawn
Dreams being rebirthed
Time being stretched out
For those running behind the curve
Freeways less packed
Conversations more rich

They say it's a pandemic
But I say it's a global reset
A chance for all the little voices to be heard
Can you hear them?

Acknowledgments

To God,

Everything that I know of love is because of You. Regardless of what human form love shows up in, I acknowledge that Your love is the source from which the purest parts of my love flow.

To my close friends,

Thank you for being present, for being a consistent love in a season of high waves and low tides. For allowing me the space to be. I Love You beyond words.

To the Muse behind the mirror,

I gotta be more careful around coffee shops...

Made in the USA
Middletown, DE
10 February 2025